Other Children

Books by Lawrence Raab

Mysteries of the Horizon
The Collector of Cold Weather
Other Children

Other Children

poems by
Lawrence Raab

Carnegie Mellon University Press
Pittsburgh 1987

Acknowledgments

The American Scholar: "Letter Home."
Antaeus: "The Moon Murders," "Empire of Lights."
The Atlantic Monthly: "In a Southern Garden."
Crazyhorse: "Romanticism," "Desire and Revenge."
The Denver Quarterly: "Scene from a Novel," "Cold Spring,"
    "Night Song," "Revision."
Iowa Review: "As If."
The Michigan Quarterly: "Two Clouds."
The New Yorker: "After Edward Hopper," "The Witch's Story."
The Ohio Review: "What We Should Have Known."
The Paris Review: "Listening to a Certain Song."
The Partisan Review: "Others."
Poetry: "The Room," "The Window," "Being Gone,"
    "Familiar Landscapes," "Afterwards," "For You," "This Day,"
    "Other Children," "Looking at Pictures," "Cloud, Castle, Lake."
Quarterly West: "On the Island," "A Familiar Story."
The Virginia Quarterly: "A Night's Museum."

"Other Children" was awarded the Bess Hokin Prize for 1983 from
    Poetry. "This Day" was also published in the Third Edition of *The
    Norton Anthology of Poetry.*
Note: Section 3 of "Empire of Lights" draws upon several passages from
    Kafka's *Diaries.* Section 9 of "Other Children" is the beginning of "The
    Juniper Tree," as translated by Lore Segal.

I would like to thank the Corporation of Yaddo, The Artists Foundation,
    Inc., The National Endowment for the Arts, and Williams College for
    their generous support.

The publication of this book is supported by grants from the National
    Endowment for the Arts in Washington, D.C., a Federal agency, and by
    the Pennsylvania Council on the Arts.

Carnegie Mellon University Press books are distributed by
    Harper and Row, Publishers.

Library of Congress Catalog Number 86-70208
ISBN 0-88748-028-4
ISBN 0-88748-029-2 Pbk.

Contents

For Judy and Jennifer

On the Island

After a night of wind we are surprised
by the light, how it flutters up from the back of the sea
and leaves us at ease. We can walk along the shore
this way or that, all day. Sit in the spiky grass
among the low whittled bushes, listening
to crickets, to the whisk of the small waves,
the rattling back of stones. "Observation,"
our Golden Nature Guide instructs, "is the key to science.
Look all around you. Some beaches
may be quite barren except for things washed up."
A buoy and a blue bottle, a lightbulb
cloudy but unbroken. For an hour
my daughter gathers trinkets, bits of good luck.
She sings the song she's just invented:
Everybody knows when the old days come.
Although it is October, today falls into the shape
of summer, that sense of languid promise
in which we are offered another
and then another spell of flawless weather.
It is the weather of Sundays,
the weather of memory, and I can see
myself sitting on a porch looking
out at water, the discreet shores
of a lake. Three or four white pines
were enough of a mystery, how they shook
and whispered, how at night I felt them
leaning against my window, like the beginning
of a story in which children must walk
deeper and deeper into a dark forest,
and are afraid, yet calm, unaware
of the arrangements made for them to survive.
My daughter counts her shells and stones,
my wife clips bayberry from the pathway. I raise

an old pair of binoculars, follow the edge of the sky
to the lighthouse, then down into the waves as they
fold around rocks humped up out of the sea.
I can turn the wheel and blur it all
into a dazzle, the pure slips and shards of light.
"A steady push of wind," we read in the book,
"gives water its rolling, rising and falling motion.
As the sea moves up and down, the wave itself
moves forward. As it nears the shore friction
from the bottom causes it to rise higher
until it tips forward in an arc and breaks."
On the table in front of the house
is the day's collection: sea-glass
and starfish, a pink claw, that blue bottle—
some to be taken home, arranged in a box,
laid on a shelf, later rediscovered, later
thrown away, casually, without regret,
and some of it, even now, to be discarded,
like the lesser stones, and the pale
chipped shells which are so alike
we can agree that saving one or two will be enough.

For You

for Judy

I don't want to say anything about
how dark it is right now, how quiet.
Those yellow lanterns among the trees,
cars on the road beyond the forest,
I have nothing to say about them.
And there's half a moon as well
that I don't want to talk about,
like those slow clouds edged
with silver, or the few unassembled stars.
There's more to all of that than this,
of course, and you would know it
better than most, better I mean
than any other, which is only
to say I had always intended
finding you here where I could
tell you exactly what I wanted to say
as if I had nothing to say
to anyone but you.

What We Should Have Known

In the movies he looks into her eyes
and knows what they both must feel.
And he's right. She feels it too,
if it's that kind of story. The hotel's
gauzy curtains billow in around them
and perhaps there are fireworks
across the piazza, or the howling
of a wolf far out on the moor.
Sometimes we can tell this scene
is just an excuse for the words
no one could manage to make believable.
I'm sure it will happen again.
Or: *Don't ask me why I mustn't marry you.*
Later, when he stares into the mirror
while shaving, he sees how badly
he's acted, wasting his life
over nothing—flimsy theories
of the perfect murder, or the experiment
that could never be reversed.
Frequently there are flashbacks
to a happier time: picnics on the beach,
boating in the park. At the end
of which he says, "I'd like
to think of you as belonging to me."
She brushes back her hair. The sun
begins to strike the hundred spires of the city.
When she walks across the lawn
we know this is the way
decisions are revealed. The breeze
ruffles her blouse, and her long white skirt
is arranged to catch hold of the light.

A Night's Museum

for Joseph Cornell

William Blake saw an angel
sitting in a tree. Blondin crossed Niagara
on a cable. And Marie Taglioni
for a Russian highwayman
danced on a panther's skin spread over the snow
in 1835. You place one marble
in the glass, one on the shelf beside it.
Five silver thimbles
become a forest, and from the chateau
romantic music exactly
like a dream. You said
you wanted to know somebody who had known Debussy.
"I could have spoken to him
and the chain
would have been established."
Blondin crossed the gorge
a second time, then a third. Many still believed
it had been done with mirrors. "So much,"
you said, "gets by me all the time
in trying to hold onto things." Far above
river, fields, and frozen woods,
against the wind a heavy cable sways.
Behind it, the star charts, the histories
of the sky like
wallpaper. And this cork ball
would be the moon,
and these
are the planets on their strings.

Romanticism

Tonight rain spills from the clogged gutters.
Say a man wakes up in the middle
of this noise, wakes up in a small room
in a hotel or a boarding house, one
of those places he has stayed in
longer than he told himself he would.
He hears the rain, and he's reminded
of some romantic vista,
then of a woman standing
on a porch, looking out, lightly
touching her hair. He tries
to remember the name of a lover from
ten years ago, but the scene
is an old postcard pasted to the glass
of a bureau, drapes frayed,
the smudged-up window looking
out on yet another building.
It passes. Let's not make him feel
too bad, or burden him
with our sorrows.
He turns over and goes back
to sleep, thinking that all of this
is what he never desired
for himself. Or he can't decide.
The rain is such evasive consolation,
spilling off the roof, just so.

Two Clouds

for Jennifer, March 20, 1977

Smallest breath
on the pillow, we counted
all the months,
first day of spring, first day
of summer, and each night now
as your silence
draws us back to you, here
where these soft leaves are leaning
over a little water
inside this circle
painted on your bed, and that cloud,
that aimless puff, goes on
floating through the same perfect sky.
If there's a secret,
I won't ask.
If there's one good explanation,
I don't want to know.
Your blue eyes
catch hold of everything
that pleases you,
and you know
what I mean when I say, *Look at that!*
That I mean, Look at me.
As if one more reckless smile
would rescue
the morning's gray
indifferent weather, and nothing
would be left to speak of
but this
feathery branch of the willow,
or the shadow of the nest
lodged above it,
or the shadow of the cloud
that sweeps the grass and is gone.

In a Southern Garden

after Bonnard

The woman who dreams, who combs her hair,
undresses, bathes, sets fruit on the table,
who stands at the mirror, or by the door,
the woman who lies in the blue expanse of her bath,
watches the window, the landscape
arranged before her, and for her.

During certain hours the light
reveals itself, green crossings
of the palms, yellow of mimosa, that sudden transparence
as she sits half-asleep in a southern garden.
The light is the subject, you said,
the light is our god.

And now the unexpected
snow on the petals of the almond trees,
and a few friends, the few who are left
to follow the coffin, pause a moment
and cannot help but see it,
all of this, as if it were still yours.

Cloud, Castle, Lake

after a story by Vladimir Nabokov

Quietly, concealing himself in his own shadow,
he followed the shore and came to a kind of inn.
Beyond it lay the blue lake, the black
parapets of a castle, and a single cloud
set also in the center of the water.

Amazed, he knew at once the promise
of that happiness which had always eluded him.
A small room for travellers was available—
red floors, the simple bed and bureau,
a mirror full of yellow flowers from the wallpaper,

and a window framing the lake
and its cloud and castle.
There was so little of his life
to change, it would not be difficult
(he decided in a moment) to resign,

and send for the few possessions he wanted—
books and a blue suit, a photograph
of the woman he had loved quite hopelessly
for the past seven years.
"I shall take it for the rest of my life,"

he said, although even then he could hear
from the far side of the lake
the cries of his fellow travellers.
They would be marching toward him,
because no one could be left behind.

And he would be made to join them
and sing the songs of the other travellers.
This tranquil scene, like such words as

"for the rest of my life," would be cast aside
and trampled underfoot, in their pleasure.

Before that afternoon he had seen glimpses
and he knew, as you must know,
how many landscapes summon us
as we pass in a train, for example,
with no hope of stopping or of turning back.

The blue dampness of a ravine.
A memory of love, disguised as a meadow.
Presented, and quickly taken back.
So unfairly, so predictably. Which was,
upon his return, all that he could tell me.

Empire of Lights

Whatever advantage the future has in size,
the past compensates for in weight, and
at their end the two are indeed no longer
distinguishable...So this circle along whose
rim we move almost closes...now we step back,
former swimmers, present walkers, and are lost.
—Franz Kafka, *Diaries*

1

Like a white cloth, slowly
unfolded and spread
over the heavy grass. Music
grown uncertain, moonlight
more indifferent. Sometimes
the unexpected cold reflects
only the lateness of the hour.
The big house afloat in its lights.
Guests, bewildered still, drifting
across the lawn, and back
to that melancholy they had always
favored. Nothing you can say
will save them. Not even
the beautiful formality
of the most difficult stories
will save them.

2

The onlookers remain
silent when the train goes past.
Another avenue
of trees, another steady
cascade of snow.
The romance of disappointment
taken to heart.
When will the new world come? they ask.
When will the repose of the dead
come about? And the wind

like a scarf laid out on the water.
Another story
we could learn to believe.

3

Are the woods still there?
The woods were still
almost there, the trees
have been growing
for twenty years. How small
should a person become
under them? Open the windows,
clear the room—the wind
blows through it. You see
only its emptiness, you search
in every corner. All these nights
in all the houses. Now you lie
against this, now against that wall,
so that the window keeps moving
around you, and this circle
almost closes.

4

Noon, afternoon,
and the aimless
grandeur of evening. Stalks of a field,
spiked and bent. Or a sway
of curtains. Or light simply
shining as if from water
on the beams of the house.
Where I sit, where I remember
certain words that still might keep
a special beauty,
as of what remains
far enough away to be seen clearly.
The moon, for example,
and the bright planets,
and the patterns of the stars.

Night Song

Out in the dark the sound
of water folding and unfolding.

On the kitchen table
plums and an apple.
The chipped white plate.
The studied poverty
of small observations.

Others are now asleep and dreaming
of strangers or the specific
fears of youth that will
by morning have left their
cloudy resemblances.

Night birds and bats.

Then a little music,
far off. Because of it
no one wakes
or changes his mind.

The yellow moon
climbs out of her clutch of branches,
serene and dispassionate,
figure from a story in which
nothing is left to chance.

Touched by that
powdery light, the real
objects of desire
darken and turn away.

A Familiar Story

When Hansel and Gretel began to eat
the house of bread and candy, an old woman
cried out, "Who is nibbling at my little house?"
And the children answered, "The wind,
the wind, the heavenly wind."

Innocent and clever, they will find the way
back home to their father, and will not blame him,
who twice agreed to send them into the woods.
There was so little to eat, and his wife
reproached him for his weakness:
"Is it better for four to starve when two might live?"

The witch's cottage was a pure temptation,
the children's lie of no importance.
"It is not me," they called.
"It is not me, but only the wind."

That night, they thought they were in heaven.
In such clean white beds
how could they help but believe in kindness?
Or imagine, as they fell asleep,
that they were home, standing together
in the kitchen doorway, the tall pines shimmering
in the sun behind them, and their real mother
kneeling in front of the oven, singing
to herself as she tested
with one finger each new loaf of bread.

Desire and Revenge

A slow fall, a long unwinding—
the Mummy's frayed white tape shredding away
as he shuffles toward us, arms
stretched out, unaccustomed even
to the dimmest candle. The leaves
brought him back, that bitter tea,
and desire, and revenge. You can't
stay dead that long and not want
to get back at someone, and that could be
anybody sitting alone in a tent
or poking around a tomb. So he stumbles out
into the light, the girl screams
and faints. She doesn't realize
she's the one he loved
hundreds of years ago,
when he was really alive. And he won't be able
to convince her now. Every time
he gets those dry fingers
around a throat, you know he's strong
but he's slow, and it seems
to occur to no one just to run away.
But we don't miss the point. It's this
close-up of the girl pressed back
against the sacrificial font, eyes
opening even wider, and then the hero
clutching his torch. And then the inevitable,
followed by a few aimless words
of explanation. As the survivors
gather their things together, the sun
blares down its blessing, and everyone
leaves, half-convinced the dead are still
angry, still in love, and sooner or later
they burn for it, unwilling
to lie down quietly, as we know
they should, and let us go.

The Moon Murders

1
"And what is that, Doctor?"

Sometimes
just the moon is enough.
Just that.

While some people take a chance
others leave it alone.
Not you, of course, but others
find themselves
carried away. And a man replies,
"I don't recall. I can't remember."
And another: "It doesn't matter."

Some people stay up all night
reading a story, watching an old movie
with no special effects.
*"Shrewd and brilliant,
he could conceal his madness
even from himself."*
As if they believed the truth
would sound like the truth.

"What's your theory, Doctor?"
*"A knot or kink
tied in the brain by some
past experience."*

2

Or just this. A tired man
turns downhill. Then everybody
starts looking for the downhill tracks.
Rain washes out the forest, and the dogs
corner him beside
another dried-out stream.

*"I couldn't sleep
so I came down here."* Sometimes the moon
is enough. When it looks
like everything else
that remains to be seen.

3

*"So I came down here
to make a more thorough examination of the body."*

Some people complain, finding this solution
difficult to believe. "A fluke," they say.
"A thousand-to-one shot." And officially
that's the story.

"What's your theory, Doctor?"
*"Locked in the human brain is a little world
all its own."*

But in reality
we're here. Where I could tell you
how the weather yesterday
seemed like a personal threat,
although it was just another
cold afternoon.

4

"And what is that, Doctor?"

*"It's a heart.
I've kept it alive for years."*

Such guarded gestures,
such small choices . . .

As if all those
very serious problems had left
only this behind: the long track
and hum of the blood
finding its way
wherever it can. Back to you,
perhaps. Or to me.

"Tell me," she asks. "What happened? I can't remember."
He smooths her hair.
She touches his hand.
"It doesn't matter."

And the moon
is climbing above the buildings,
above the chilly lake, above the fields,
one after another.

The Witch's Story

Everything you have heard about me
is true, or true enough.
You shouldn't think
I'd change my story now.
A stubborn, willful little girl
comes sneaking
around my house, peering
in all the windows. She's disobeyed
her parents, who knew
where the witch lived. "If you go,
you're not our daughter any more."
That's what they told her. I have
my ways of knowing. All pale
and trembly then, she knocks at my door.
"Why are you so pale?"
I ask, although of course
I know that too.
She'd seen what she'd seen—
a green man on the stairs, and the other one,
the red one, and then the devil himself
with his head on fire, which was me,
the witch in her true ornament, as I
like to put it. Oh, she'd seen what she needed
to send her running home
but she walked right in, which is the part
I never understand completely. Maybe
she believed, just then,
that she was no one's daughter any more,
and had to take her chances, poor thing,
inside with me. "So you've come
to brighten up my house,"
I said, and changed her into a log.
It was an easy trick, and gave me little pleasure.

But I'd been waiting all day.
I was cold, and even that
small fire was bright, and warm enough.

Scene from a Novel

In this scene from the novel
you just started, a father
tiptoes into his daughter's room
to watch her sleeping. All he wants
is to look at her for a moment.
He brushes the damp hair from her eyes,
touches her unfolded hand so that
she murmurs and turns against the pillows.
The room is streaked with yellow
from the night-light. Careful stacks
of books beside the bed, favorite animals
pushed up against the wall,
and the sheets all ruffled and apart.
You know what he's thinking—the apparent
safety of the house, the inevitable damages.
Turning the page, you grow more apprehensive.
Suspecting what will happen
chapters later, you can't help but resent
this cruel preparation. Yet each night
fathers step into such rooms
long after it's time to say goodnight
and feel implicated and afraid.

As If

It isn't as if you had to sit there
in the grass, watching whatever
it is you would say you are watching.

Some flowers. The daisies, the others
whose names you never learned.
Or the birds—the bluejay, the robin.

It isn't as if you had to feel this way.
The stem of the daisy is slender and pale,
furred with jagged little leaves.

The frill of petals, of course,
is white, and reminds us
of who loves us, who does not.

We'd all rather be happy,
wouldn't we? You just aren't sure
if remembering the names would help.

The oak, the elm, and the willow.
And the other people you can see
who are so busy with their lives,

it isn't as if you could be certain
they are happy, it isn't
as if you could ask them, mentioning

only the weather, how it is likely
to change by evening, how it is likely
to remain the same.

Others

You will not appear in this story.
I won't find you strolling casually
in the little grove of ash and elm.
When the door opens, that will be my wife
returning from her shopping, my daughter
dancing in her new sneakers. Today
no ghosts will be allowed to arrive
wrapt in their mild shimmers of light.

Nor you, who have so often entered
these stories, speaking
my lines, accepting my instructions
with that perfectly insubstantial
attention that becomes you
amid all of this ordinary life.

I walk out to get the mail,
drive to school, to the store.
I see a movie and returning home
glance up at the stars.
I sit down to write, and the stillness
begins to make me wish for you,

but I will give you nothing
to think of, not even the smallest
memory of a child
blurred and held high in his father's arms—
that imperfect light in which my father
holds and steadies me, and my mother
tells us to be still and look
in her direction, then pushes
the shutter, jarring the camera slightly,
a simple maneuver she would never master.

If you were here I would ask you
to turn and walk away, knowing
you'd have no choice and would believe me
if I told you I'd made all of this up
to pass the time, as it has,
regardless. And now

my house is so quiet
what I imagine most clearly
is my wife and daughter turning
in their sleep upstairs,
and now I believe I can hear
their breathing, so precise
and thoughtless,
so easy to mistake for my own.

For my mother, Marjorie Young Raab
October 10, 1913—March 20, 1978

The Room

Everything has been arranged too carefully.
The way the eyes are closed, that certainty.
I can see it isn't possible to pretend
that the dead are only sleeping.
The way the hands are folded
we don't have to touch them.
When I touched them I knew it wasn't necessary.
I've watched my wife and daughter sleeping.
I've watched you. No matter how still,
there's an imperceptible trembling
accompanies everything that lives.
It's the way a feather sways, that chance.
It's the cloud on the mirror,
that stain. For a while we imagined
our concerns were yours. Is this blue dress
the one you would have wanted to wear?
And these rings, that silver pin?
Is this the music you especially liked to hear?
But the dead among their flowers
have no preferences, and I think
it must be wrong to pretend otherwise,
if only for my sake, and not now for yours.

The Window

The gold spires of the poplars—
this is the day's reflection.
It is what you see when
you look out of the window,
what I see. Clouds
cross and darken them.
Behind them the pines mass.
All of this passes.
Tomorrow, thinking of something else,
I won't notice a thing—
not the shine of the bark,
not the sway of the darker branches.
At night the window
returns the edge of the table,
a shoulder and a sleeve.
Without thinking, I trust that small
invisible landscape, its daily
withdrawal, that has nothing to do
with me, or any of us who remain.
It's the only way. Maybe
you would have said so too,
would have written it
in the margin of a book, as I,
trusting your presence,
waited elsewhere, writing
about those trees, thinking
of no one in particular.
You always knew
when I wanted to be alone.
But not now. That's all
I'd like to tell you.

Familiar Landscapes

1

Morning's sudden and extravagant
green seems to suggest the higher
whiter waves of the air, what moves
through the flurry of these
first leaves, floating and falling
beyond everything I am able to see.
Against that brightness, a flock of blue,
a single yellow iris
creaks on its shaft. How persistently
the eye resists the familiar,
so easily finding itself content
among its accustomed walls,
the expected trees and avenues,
that it fails to see them
and will acknowledge
only what has been changed or lost
or taken away.

2

The mountain darkens with the sky
and the quiet lake
holds onto the light as long as it can.
That's the way we looked at it
one summer. The shadowed lane.
The silence of the house.
Sometimes a few words are all we ask for
and it's too much.
With the tube down your throat
you couldn't talk. "Not to be able
to breathe for yourself," the young doctor
told my father, "that's the worst thing
to take away from anyone."

41

3

Even the most familiar landscape
opens itself to the moon's cold
inspection, and is changed.
Dreaming all night, waking
early, I'm unable to remember
what appeared essential
only a moment ago, an image
perhaps, or a fact that asked
something of me
just because it was there, now
lost altogether in the day's
advances—this absolute blue
against which the wind displays
these clouds as they drift
and gather, shred,
rise, and are carried away.

Afterwards

I wasn't thinking of you.
But so much stays the same.
Even a room resists our efforts.
The old things are taken away,
given away, lost. A new chair,
a different picture. Entering,
I expect you to be there.

These are the inescapable
phrases that hope for more:
something about the weather,
and all that can and cannot
be healed, and how, and how long.
Time passes, and it reminds us
of everything we happen to remember.

Then we return to the same
few objects, few events. The house
darkens, and the lights come on.
And even this room
changes to fit your absence,
no matter what we say or how
we choose to think about it.

Being Gone

We wouldn't have to see so much.
The light could pass us by.
But it would hesitate
the way it will on water,
on the bluest stretch of water,
as if it knew us better
than we say we know ourselves.
We wouldn't have to see it go.
And we would have no more
of the cold to wait for,
no more of the wind
jangling its trees
or the snap of the snow
as a man in a field
in the blue dazzle of the snow
pulls his heavy coat a little closer.
Nor would we care so much
for all of this
that we turn to, touching
as if for the last time
whatever is at hand.

This Day

Watching the beautiful
sticks of trees as they click and sway,
the first green unravelling,

it's easy to imagine I might
remember this day forever.
I say it to myself,

never to others, while the poem
made hoping to preserve it
is changed, then changed again

to fit another order
it happens to discover.
At the end I find myself

in a room by a window, or at the edge
of a field, with the same clear
sky above me wherein later

I will imagine clouds, as if
some movement were required. That,
or a different kind of stillness.

So there must also be
a family circled round
the bedside of someone

who is dying. I place
myself among them.
All of us are waiting

for the little we believe we need
to hold on to and repeat.
But this is not my family

although it is you
who are dying, your words
I am again unable to imagine

as everything continues
sliding together in the light,
that day so easily

changed to this one,
the sky that is so blue, and the clouds
that cross my gaze with such terrible speed.

4

After Edward Hopper

Usually it is night
but always there are windows.
And the green shades
in the rooms of small hotels
drawn halfway.
The carafe of water
on a heavy bureau.
And the woman
taking off her clothes.

The letter on the bed
beneath a picture of the ocean.
The yellow windows of the buildings.
Halfway through the afternoon
trees are drawn
to the edge of a field, and the light
in the rooms of houses by the sea
is still
almost perfectly white.

Cold Spring

The last few gray sheets of snow are gone,
winter's scraps and leavings lowered
to a common level. A sudden jolt
of weather pushed us outside, and now
this larger world once again belongs to us.
I stand at the edge of it, beside the house,
listening to the stream we haven't heard
since fall, and I imagine one day thinking
back to this hour and blaming myself
for my worries, my foolishness, today's choices
having become the accomplished
facts of change, accepted
or forgotten. The woods are a mangle
of lines, yet delicate, yet precise,
when I take the time to look closely.
If I'm not happy it must be my own fault.
At the edge of the lawn my wife
bends down to uncover a flower, then another.
The first splurge of crocuses.
And for a moment the sweep and shudder
of the wind seems indistinguishable
from the steady furl of water
just beyond her.

Letter Home

This afternoon I saw a deer inside that narrow
strip of woods between the rose gardens
and the Northway. She bolted, paused, turned
twice. I wasn't going to move much closer,
and I was willing to feel like the intruder.
But the noise she made dismissed me—
two chuffs of annoyance or disgust.
And then on the road back three groundhogs
in the long grass heard me coming and rushed
beneath the cottage. Jennifer, I think
you would have laughed out loud to see
their lopsided, ungainly waddle—
foolish creatures, and not designed
to hurry gracefully. But I imagine
fear was what they really felt.
Someone who knows more about these things
might tell us even that's too human
a word to work exactly. One sound
that doesn't fit—my heavy step
on the path—triggers the instinct to escape,
and afterwards what passes
for the usual allows their tentative return.
Also I know the birds don't sing for gladness,
although it's hard not to want to think so
when we're happy. Which is also to suggest
that the big smile you inscribe upon the sun,
saying, each time you explain a picture,
"Look, it has a face," makes that face your own
laughing kindly back at you, and sometimes
I choose to believe it's mine as well.

Listening to a Certain Song

tonight I was reminded of our house in England,
the little record player that always skipped.
Our dozen records seemed such a luxury, although
we had much more back home in Massachusetts.
I don't want to pretend that we were poor.
You read Virginia Woolf and Thomas Hardy.
We argued badly and often about whether
or not to have a child, and when you cried
I talked until you stopped, with nothing settled
and nothing proven except that so many words
might bring us back to the way I thought
our lives should be. Twice it snowed.
Birds nested in the thatched roof. A woman
we never saw again brought us a Christmas tree
with the roots still on it. When we show
the photographs of that house to friends
it's this we talk about—the deer in the woods,
the cow that got loose on the lawn. Remember
waiting once a week for the bus to market day?
Remember when the rented car broke down in Scotland?
How easily that year becomes this landscape
of favorite stories, revised out of habit until
neither of us can tell whose correction
is the truth, or if it really matters.
Friends drove down from London, nervous
and unhappy, their marriage a wreck,
and worse to come. We gathered blackberries
from the hedgerows until the neighbors
must have thought we were starving
and brought us loaves of bread, unable
to make sense of Americans who didn't own a car.
But no one can ever understand why anyone
chooses to live where they're living.

I told the man who sold me rubber boots
that I liked the silence. "Ah yes!" he replied.
"But sometimes the silence can drive you mad."
And we laughed at his dramatic gesture because
the silence was wonderful and no one
either of us had known
had ever gone mad. We bought a chair that broke
and a lot of books we sent home in small, carefully
wrapped packages, and they all arrived.

Far Away and Near

Like the pleasure of a riddle
what matters is the hour
spent in the dark inventing a solution

impossible to resolve.
White complications: like a tablecloth
in a still life by Cezanne,

how it resembles a mountain as
I watch it become one.
Or the trees so much like light

they might as well be floating.
Then the persistent weight of the stone.
What astonishes us?

"It is the reflection which *envelops*,"
said Cezanne. Also
a certain amount of blue

is necessary to give
"the impression of air."
A few blue lines

disappear into the maze which
indicates branches. The paper's
a blank field of light, inviting

us closer but keeping
the distance we know is required.
There were never any secrets,

just pine trees and boulders,
fruit on a table,
whatever he saw.

Looking at Pictures

A narrow path snaking along the cliff's edge,
that cold garden with its clipped hedges
and heavy flowers, even the cottage in the forest
—our car by the gate, you somewhere inside—
don't look enough like the places
where we were, although these pictures
are the proof we turn to
and show our friends. This is a good one,
I say—clear blue light and the mist dividing
hillside from hillside, so the eye
moves slowly upward to that castle
or church, at the center. And this
is the village where we lived for a week.
This is the house by the sea.
Then another duplicate cliff and sweep
of water, black flecks of birds like flaws
in an inch of sky, and the wind bending things down.
It became a sweet joke: all those ancient rocks
and the sea crashing against them.
Sometimes you are standing on the pathway,
sometimes there is only the landscape we came for,
my eye squinting into the viewfinder,
then the definite snap of the shutter.
I kept imagining how it all
would appear later, and what I'd find
myself remembering—the pressure each day
of merely looking, the desire to have felt
more than I would feel?
Or perhaps that was later, and as we walked
on a little further that afternoon
we were talking about the weather, or where
to buy groceries for the weekend, a newspaper,
a map, the ordinary details, the brief

consistent present, which is always lost.
I held up the camera.
The real wind pulled at my arms.
Waves were sweeping across the channel.

Revision

The moment I expected, like the stories
I had read before, always
left the dying a few minutes to say
what was most important, and sometimes
there were six months or a year
in which to arrange the best departure,
invent the necessary
final words, and correct them.

*

I think this must be
what a writer depends on,
the chance to change his mind, time enough
to risk the initial embarrassments
of feeling. And all the clumsy stabs
at wind, trees, clouds, water, however
poorly made are still essential and allow
for the better, more believable
lines that follow.

*

I once confessed to friends in college
how I hoped to discover
I'd been adopted. What did I want?
Another kind of exile,
perhaps, more serious and substantial
than leaving home. We'd been reading
Joyce's *Portrait,* and we were smart enough
to know that Stephen wasn't Joyce exactly.
Then I believed that writing
was the way to invent everything

that hadn't happened to me, as if
in preparation for a truer life
I would later claim as my own.

*

That sudden heart attack
denied us my mother's final words.
We stood around the bed. We didn't know
if she could hear what we were saying.
Driving to the funeral,
I started to cry because I couldn't
recall clearly enough the last day
we'd spent together. I'd felt
sick, slept all afternoon
in my room, said little.
Like a child I wanted it back again,
just that day, to do it over.
But even as my wife assured me
everything had been all right, I hadn't
acted badly, and I held on
to the wheel of the car, I knew
that nothing I could
make or remake
would leave me what I wanted.

Other Children

1

When my daughter watched the explosion
of Mount St. Helens on the evening news,
and saw those houses smashed by the mudslides,
she could not have known this wasn't
likely to happen here, and she was worried,
for the first time perhaps, over such concerns—
someone's house crushed and gone completely,
someone's father breaking down and sobbing,
who had just been told for certain what he'd lost.

Nor could she have understood how often
we'd seen that shot, that man
among the wreckage, a broken toy in his hand.
Nor, at three years old, could she
have expected that he was going to cry—
covering his face with both his hands
as if embarrassed by his grief—and then
look up, bewildered, at us.

2

Accustomed to the daily
summaries of loss, it's easy to believe
the news, by definition, happens elsewhere,
and in a world that's always worse
than it is, each day, for us.

But when I watch my wife and daughter
drive off to school, sometimes I can't
help but see myself standing beside
the warped and twisted metals of the car.
Inside, they're looking up
at nobody. And I can't move away
from the edge of this imagining,

where no one calls me,
or comes crawling out of that fire.

3

In Grimm's "The Juniper Tree," the perfect,
beautiful wife wanted a child so badly
she died of happiness when he was born,
and then was buried, as she had asked,
beneath that tree. But the stepmother
envied the boy and one afternoon
when he was looking inside a chest
to find an apple, she slammed the lid
down on his neck, and his head flew off.
Now what will I do? she thought.
She picked him up and set his head back on,
put an apple in his hands, and when
her own daughter, Ann Marie, returned
from school, she said, "Go ask your brother
to share the apple I just gave him,
and if he doesn't answer, box his ears."
The girl went off and did as she was told,
then ran back sobbing. "O Ann Marie,
what have you done? But we will stew him
in the sour broth, and no one will know."
So the woman cut him up and served
that black stew to her husband,
who couldn't help but eat, saying,
"What good food this is! Give me more."
And the more he ate the more he wanted.

4

In the newspapers I read about a father
who put his son in a bathtub filled
with scalding water because
the child needed to be taught a lesson.

So much that seems essential
is simply not included.

And this: in California
a young woman named Betty Lansdown Fouquet
left her five-year-old daughter out to die
on the center divider of the interstate.
Twelve hours later, when the girl
was rescued by the highway patrol,
they had to pry her fingers from the Cyclone fence.
She told them she had run after
the car which was carrying her stepfather,
her brother and sister, and her mother,
"for a long time."

5

But Ann Marie saved her brother's bones,
tied them in her scarf, and laid them
in the grass under the juniper.
All at once that tree began to tremble,
and a bird flew out of the branches, singing
so sweetly no one could resist, even
the stepmother had to go outside
to hear it, and a millstone fell on her head
and she was crushed. From that spot
fire rose. When it was gone the bird was gone,
the brother was restored, and he took his father
and sister by their hands, and they went back
inside the house, sat down and ate their supper.

6

Driving to work one morning a man
sees this little girl running right along
the divider by the chain link fence.
He's half a mile down the road before
he gets angry that her parents would let her
play in a place so dangerous. Some people,
he thinks, shouldn't be allowed to have kids.
Then he can't imagine how she crossed
the lanes to get there, but tells himself
there's got to be an explanation even if
he's now too far away to find out what.
Later, at home, he doesn't tell his wife
the story, worried she might ask him
if he stopped, and he would have to tell her
how he couldn't, not at that hour,
with all that traffic, which she should understand,
but he knows she wouldn't understand.

7

"When I die," my daughter asked me,
"will I still have my fingers?"
I can't remember what I told her.
That day I must have thought
any answer would be sufficient.

Some stories seem impossible
to explain with any other story.
The boy in the bathtub, the girl
running along the divider,
her brother and her sister watching
from the back seat of the car as if,
perhaps, they were the ones who needed
to be taught a lesson. What kind of shape
would hold this, even briefly, all together,
with no magical bird, and without its song?

As my family sleeps I step outside and see
the early morning air glittering
in the arms of the pines, and clouds
lifting from the mountain into a sky
already clear and weightless,
while on the lawn in the frost
each shrub and tree has laid its own
brief white ghost.

8

Let's say the boy survives, is sent away
to live with a family who always wanted
a child to care for. Years later
he receives this letter: *All that I desire
now in my life is for you to forgive me,
but if you can't I know I will understand.*

Or the little girl grows up and marries,
has a daughter of her own and for a time
she's happy, until her husband
leaves her, one morning, for no reason
she can figure out. His note says only,
Got to get away for a while.
Will write soon and try to send some money.
But he doesn't write, and no matter
what she does her child keeps crying
until all she can think about is how
to keep her from crying.

9

It is a long time ago now, as much as two thousand years maybe, that there was a rich man and he had a wife and she was beautiful and good, and they loved each other very much but they had no children even though they wanted some so much, the wife prayed and prayed for one both day and night, and still they did not and they did not get one. In front of their house was a yard and in the yard stood a juniper tree. Once, in wintertime, the woman stood under the tree and peeled herself an apple, and as she was peeling the apple she cut her finger and the blood fell onto the snow. "Ah," said the woman and sighed a deep sigh, and she looked at the blood before her and her heart ached. "If I only had a child as red as blood and as white as snow." And as she said it, it made her feel very happy, as if it was really going to happen.

10

One by one the bones are gathered.
Not even the smallest is left behind.
Such care is taken that when the body returns
it will not lack a finger or a toe.
Mist rises, spreads, and blurs the landscape.
Later it will rain. Later the sun
will rise, the morning's haze burn off, and birds
assemble once again in the juniper. Years
will pass, and the bones will grow still whiter
waiting for the body to come back to them.
Other children will be born, some loved,
some feared. And the parents who loved them
will find their places in the ground beside
the ones who did not, as the wind flutters
the branches of the tree, the birds repeat
their most familiar notes, and some who listen
imagine they can sense a shape beneath
this song, which for a time contains the grief
each believed was his, or hers, alone.